Foreword

First of all, thank you, Betty, for recognizing and then writing the story to acknowledge the amazing courage and love that prompted Rob and Sharon to take on the raising of eleven children who needed a loving home. I admire them for willingly parenting—again—at their age and pray for them day by day.

Betty, you have done a good job of helping us to journey with them through your written account. They certainly have not had an easy road, or an easy load. The financial involvement alone would make anyone planning toward retirement flinch. Their faith and obedience have been a great example for us all.

I have not had the privilege of meeting the eleven except through a delightful letter of introduction. Each of these child-persons are individual, different, and precious to the family and to God who personally fashioned them. Rob and Sharon—and the many, many people who have supported them in countless ways—have the opportunity to be a part of the process of who each one will become. An awesome privilege and responsibility! May God bless each parent, each child, and the many people whose lives will also be touched because one or another of these eleven were a part of their world.

Rob and Sharon, you have done a great thing—and you are continuing to do such an important and amazing thing for the benefit of many! God be with you.

—Janette Steeves Oke

Janette Oke (nee Steeves) is a longtime beloved Canadian author of inspirational fiction, with more than seventy-five books under her belt. The television series *When Calls the Heart* is based on her novel by that name. She is also Rob Steeves's cousin. She may be retired now, but her prayerful support remains.

STRONG
11

Adventures in Faith and Adoption

Betty Barkman

ISBN: 978-1-4866-2577-2
eBook ISBN: 978-1-4866-2578-9

Word Alive Press
119 De Baets Street Winnipeg, MB R2J 3R9
www.wordalivepress.ca

WORD ALIVE
—P R E S S—

Cataloguing in Publication information can be obtained from Library and Archives Canada.

This story – of my friend Sharon and her husband Rob's adoption journeys to the Ukraine - is one that must be told. Not only told but read, with open heart and eyes. There are orphans out there waiting for us to come.

Are you not curious who our Father might call or why? Are you not wondering what such an adventure could look like for you? The truth is our Father calls each of us for something.

My friends' story will take you along on an incredible journey as they step out, never fully knowing what is ahead yet they trust and believe; they engage in unbelievable warfare, whether climbing mountains or waiting quietly when hope falters. Prayers are answered, miracles keep happening, orphanage gates get opened; such things can happen only through our Father's loving hands. You see the magnitude of their obedient yes when you groan with them in the life and death struggle for one of their new daughters.

Every child adopted changes a life but that change keeps multiplying and will change upcoming generations…

Sharon and I met in the middle of the border closing to come in and out of Ukraine. (I had to leave without our two little girls because the court proceedings had not been done in time.) We stayed in contact, encouraging &

praying for each other. We share our love for the children and following our Father when He calls us, however crazy or impossible it may seem. We both were older when God called us to this step of obedience.

Please read my friends' story and let God speak to your heart as He unfolds and reveals His heart in their journey. As you read, watch Him reveal His heart for your journey as well, as you too step out in faith . . .

Blessings Cindy

Cindy and her husband Dennis Boyer live in Brooksville, Florida. They have been on their own adoption journeys both to Ukraine and Russia where they still have a daughter to love from afar. In their home they currently have seven children aged 8 to 18, all adopted from the Ukraine.

Rob and Sharon.

PART ONE

The Saga Begins

2016–2017

With his chin in his hands, elbows anchored on his knees, and staring into space, Declan sat on the stoop of the cracked and weatherbeaten brown brick building behind him. He had been doing some serious thinking—as serious as any five-year-old boy can.

Is it true? he wondered. *Is there really a God out there? Somewhere?*

Never before had he heard of such a thing.

He craned his neck forward, vainly trying to peer farther into the skies, wishing for just one tiny glimpse of Him, whoever He was. Then he would know.

But the light was fading. It was useless. Any minute now— as always, far too soon—the group leader would be hollering "Bedtime!"

• • •

Half a world away, right in the centre of Canada, Sharon and her husband Rob were getting nice and comfortable. God had been amazingly good to them. They participated in a good church. Their country home and its acreage were developing beautifully. Their nursing jobs, which had once seemed so demanding, were paying off well. Their savings account was growing, and this showed in some of the things they had been able to do recently. After a thirteen-year absence, they'd gotten to enjoy a very pleasant although emotional reunion with Sharon's family in Ireland. And finally, they'd taken a few trips just for fun. They'd recently gone to Cuba with their youngest son Peter as a Christmas vacation.

Their family—yes, their large blended family, with all nine children plus grands—was doing great lately.

The word *blended* startled Sharon, momentarily, and stopped her short in the midst of making a thank-you list during a time of reflection. Their lives hadn't been easy. Life would never be perfect, not exactly. But they had come so far.

The next word that jumped out at her, and not for the first time, was *undeserving*.

Yes, we are so undeserving.

It was true. Their track record had blemishes. Both she and Rob were in their second marriages and the ugliness in the early stories was best left alone. But there had also been so much grace and forgiveness. God believed in second chances. That was always her anchor, one she came back to and clung to for dear life no matter how many times the enemy snuck in to batter her soul.

Unexpectedly, she felt a nibbling at her heart that she couldn't explain. Did God want something more, something else of them? Undeserving people like her and Rob didn't get called into anything special, did they?

The nibble didn't budge. Instead it grew. And strangely, it felt like God was behind it. Was He really? What did He want? How would they know?

• • •

Declan couldn't believe it.

The worker—her name was Viktoria, he had just found out—said it again, and this time it almost made sense. Viktoria was adamant. It sounded like she was telling the truth.

"There is a God, a real God," she said. "He sees you. He's watching over you. He knows you by name. He loves you."

Really? he thought. *All eighteen of us forgotten kids in my group alone, in this crumbly old place? Never mind all the other groups? He sees us all? How come no one ever told us? How come...*

But there was more.

"And you can pray to Him," Viktoria added. "He likes to hear His children pray to Him. You can tell Him about stuff and ask Him for things…"

Hmmm.

Now Declan was intrigued. No, he was hooked. This, he would pursue. And he knew without a shadow of a doubt what he would pray for. He'd been at this orphanage since he was two. As far back as he could remember, all he had wanted in life was one thing.

If he was a little braver, he would ask Viktoria to explain things and perhaps answer some of his questions.

But maybe he should check with his sister, Niamh. She was older. Would she know more about it?

It turned out that Niamh didn't know a lot more, but she did have a somewhat better grasp of things, and for now that would have to be enough.

They agreed. They may not have any privacy to call their own, but this one thing they could do. Every day, for as long as it took, they would pray for the only item on their wish list: a mom and a dad. And if they should get a chance to tell Conor, who was in a different home now, he would surely join them.

• • •

The small group Rob and Sharon attended was studying the book *Crazy Love* by Frances Chan. Week after week, new questions came up. "Would you be willing to do something crazy just because you love Jesus, if He asked you to?" The answers didn't come readily.

One week, the leader said, "Tell me what you're thinking. What crazy things could we be doing for Jesus?"

"We could adopt a child," Sharon blurted out without thinking.

Everyone turned to stare at her, including Rob.

"And have ten children instead of nine?" he queried in disbelief.

Embarrassed, she laughed. "I'm only kidding. Only kidding."

Of course she was only kidding. She was already fifty and Rob was four years older.

• • •

Rob's dad out in Edmonton, Alberta needed to have open heart surgery with quadruple bypass. Naturally, Rob and Sharon decided to go. While there, in early September, they stayed with Rob's sister Debbie, who had been very involved in a children's ministry that summer. She eagerly showed Sharon a new DVD that featured three happy children who'd recently been adopted cross-culturally.

Sharon was intrigued enough to ask for permission to view it again later with Rob.

After seeing the video together, they stared at each other for a long moment but didn't talk about it. Not then.

• • •

One night Sharon had a vision—not that she knew what a vision was. She'd never had one before and certainly didn't consider herself prone to such strange things.

But she could think of no better way to explain it.

She saw a thin but attractive-looking young girl walk toward her with arms outstretched. Although she couldn't immediately derive its meaning, the picture was crystal clear, all the way to the colour of the girl's hair and the detailed style of her almost-shapeless dress, hanging loosely on her much-too-skinny frame.

The picture stayed with her, haunting her. No way could she keep this to herself. Together, she and Rob speculated on the meaning of it, both that night and many nights after.

• • •

Declan never found out why Viktoria, the wonderful worker who had talked about God, disappeared as quickly as she'd arrived. An older kid told him that she had only been a "temporary" and needed to go wherever she was told. Maybe she was working in a different orphanage now. He didn't know.

Declan wished she'd stayed longer. He had a sneaky feeling that maybe she had gotten into trouble for talking about God. In her absence, should he keep praying like she had told them to? Was what she'd said still true?

He had no proof, and now no encouragement, yet something told him to keep it up.

Yes. Niamh agreed with Declan. They couldn't lose.

They didn't see a single speck of opportunity around them, but they weren't going to take a chance by quitting now, just in case this God-story was real. It was their only hope.

And so, except for those odd days when discouragement overpowered their resolution, the two of them kept at it, day after day after day—in the dark, on their knees, beside their cots, after the lights were out.

As orphanages go, theirs wasn't all that bad. Declan didn't know anything else.

Aren't kids meant to be mostly skin and bones? he asked himself. *Don't apples always have worms? Don't all children get yelled at, slapped, and then sent to bed without food when they spill something at the table? Aren't all playgrounds built on mud and feature equipment that was meant for two but stretched out for twenty? Or for a hundred?*

These things were probably all normal. None of them were big issues, either, as far as Declan could tell. They certainly wouldn't matter once his prayers got answered.

He could hardly wait. Might it possibly be soon?

• • •

Once Sharon and Rob lined up the nuggets—the nudging, the crazy love question, the DVD, the vision—they knew without a doubt that God wanted their attention. They listened and began immediately to put their thoughts into action. Somehow they both knew that they were supposed to go to Ukraine to adopt a child. Nothing specific pointed to this—just the deep knowing that they knew that they knew, an experience that comes often to God-followers.

But the nitty-gritty of such an amazing project soon felt overwhelming. The size of it, the fear, the expense, the unanswered questions… my goodness, this was way more than they had bargained for.

Yet they persisted.

"If God is calling us to this thing, He will surely make a way," they reminded each other. "Our part is simply to obey."

So they slogged through the many hassles. How many police checks, house checks, government letters, office visits, and extended delays would it take?

And how much money?

"If we had known early on exactly how much it would cost us, we would certainly have chickened out," Sharon said later. "But tactfully God hid that from us until our hearts were deeply involved."

They sold their truck and camper and drained their precious bank account. Sill, it wasn't enough.

Really, Lord? they prayed. *Surely $50,000 should have done it, shouldn't it?*

And their careers? They'd have to be gone for an extended time. In fact, an unknown length of time, they were told quite adamantly. No firm dates could be set. The Ukrainian government demanded that adoptive parents remain present during the entire final processes. And, as it was rapidly becoming clear to them, these people had a penchant for creating unforeseen delays.

Thankfully, Sharon's and Rob's employers were understanding and gracious. Their positions as nurses would be held for them until they returned.

Somewhere, somehow, their plan to adopt one child evolved into the possibility of taking several. They didn't plan it that way; it just happened in their hearts. God alone knows how it happened.

But really, what if there were siblings at the orphanage who needed to stay together? Maybe two or three or four?

Somehow their heart settled on a number—three. This is what they prepared for and applied for and qualified for.

Three siblings it would be.

• • •

On their long overseas flight, Rob couldn't resolve the worry that haunted him most.

"How in the world will we decide which ones we want?" he asked Sharon.

They had been told that they couldn't make their choice beforehand, nor could they wait until they saw the children and then decide which ones clicked with them. No. In an office in the city, before they got to any orphanages, they would be presented with a file with pictures of all the available children, possibly hundreds, and they would have to make their choice then and there before proceeding.

"That's impossible," he fumed as the sleepless hours slowly ticked by. "How can we pick a few and discard all the others?"

Sharon could only shake her head. The peace of God could be tangible, she knew, but it could also seem fragile and elusive.

Together they bowed their heads one more time to commit their unanswerable question to God. Surely He would show them a way, wouldn't He?

Even then, peace was tentative.

• • •

The moment arrived. After all the connections and shuttles and taxis and buses and narrow streets and huge old buildings—and lovely, ornate ones, too—these two foreigners sat in front of a desk across from a solemn-faced official. She stared at them and pushed forward the dreaded files.

"Take your time," she said through an interpreter.

With that, she left them to it.

Sharon and Rob made eye contact. *Can we do this? Are we ready?* Behind these unspoken words was the lingering fear, but also the trust that sought hard to override it.

Slowly, ever so slowly, Rob pulled the big file forward. He let it open wherever it would. He had no plan, no vision of how this might go.

Sharon looked down and gasped.

"Huh?" Rob said.

"That's her," she finally sputtered. "That's the one I saw."

The very first picture they stared at was the picture Sharon had seen in her vision. A perfect replica down to the last detail.

Just like that, they never needed to make that painful decision. God had already made it for them and shown them months before.

"God, this is incredible," Rob said. "Help my unbelief. You knew right along who You had picked and I didn't get it."

"And does she have siblings?" Sharon asked.

The woman nodded. "She does. Two brothers. If you choose this girl, you'll have to take all three."

Wow! And God had known that, too.

• • •

Declan felt as puzzled as Niamh. Conor had come, too. Strange. How had he gotten here? And why? His group lived a mile away. What had they done wrong?

Children were never called to the director's office unless they were in trouble.

• • •

This was a once in a lifetime moment for Sharon and Rob, one that would be forever engraved on their hearts. They watched as their children entered the room for the first time.

The moment felt earth-shattering. When the person in charge asked the three children if they wanted these two visitors to be their parents—aided by interpreters, of course—each of their faces showed the comprehension of the offer. They eyes widened and their mouths hung open as it dawned on them. Their expressions changed gradually to delight as they nodded their heads and spilled out a unified, resounding "Yes!"

This new family couldn't understand each other, but the twinkle in the kids' eyes spoke louder than words. They were giving God a thumbs up.

Sharon and Rob needed no prompting. With arms outstretched, they invited the three forward. Within seconds, they were all cuddling together on the sofa. Declan crawled up into Sharon's lap and hugged her tight. It was the never-want-to-let-you-go kind of tight.

"Can we call you Mama and Papa?" one of the children asked.

Really? Within the first five or ten minutes?

God, this is truly beyond words, Sharon thought.

• • •

That first meeting occurred on December 8, 2016. The process had begun.

Sharon and Rob stayed at the Fiesta Hotel, three kilometres from the orphanage. They'd been taken by car that first day, together with interpreters. Afterward they were on their own. They decided that walking shouldn't be a problem, not to mention a good way to keep in shape. Rob had always been good at finding his way around strange places, so he was quite confident.

Yet that first day he got humiliatingly disoriented and they found themselves hopelessly lost. After an urgent plea for help, a gallant rescue, and a late arrival, he vowed that it would never happen again.

It didn't.

They had daily appointments to be with the children for an hour or more. In no time at all, the children at the orphanage started to come up to them and chatter—in Russian, of course—while others dashed off to tell Declan and his siblings, "Your Papa and Mama are here."

Every day, they brought along healthy treats, whether it be fruit or popcorn, and occasionally they'd bring a gift, like a teddy bear. They all played together during these visits, usually outside, and often worked up a sweat. The children and their friends had energy!

Sometimes all this play built intrigue. One day, with lots of fresh snow on the ground, Rob and Sharon decided to build a snowman. They got everyone involved, including their own kids' surprised friends. Finding helpful items from debris lying around, like an abandoned tire, the children gathered pinecones and twigs which they soon displayed proudly on a beautiful snowman standing more than six feet tall.

During all this fun, they noticed two workers watching shrewdly, their expressions hard to read. Had they never heard of snowmen? Or had they never seen adults play happily with kids?

This playtime seemed to have been arranged for Rob and Sharon to get to know their children; if they were to reconsider the whole thing, they would have to get out now.

But they never toyed with that option. To them, this was a done deal.

One by one, though, the kids started acting up, trying their new parents' patience. This was unpleasant but not unexpected; Rob and Sharon had been duly warned.

• • •

The night of December 11 was a strange one. Rob and Sharon had enjoyed their best yet visit with the children. After agreeing on their carefully laid plans, they returned to the hotel thinking that they were ready for whatever came next.

Around midnight, Rob and Sharon were hustled into a twelve-passenger van. The driver seemed to be in a rush, never mind the deep potholes, and neither he nor their adoption worker spoke English.

They soon found themselves back at the orphanage, where the children stood waiting on the stoop with another worker. Soon they were all off to Kyiv to get immigration medicals for the children.

The impatient driver, speeding along, got them there early, at 6:30 a.m. Their appointment was set for eight o'clock.

After a string of tests, including urine samples, X-rays, and countless trips up and down numerous flights of stairs, all that remained was one final visit to the doctor. Older and abrupt, this woman sounded like a general barking orders in Russian. The kids were pretty scared of her, but soon, after a final correction on their Canadian embassy papers, everything was done.

"Done," Rob said with a grimace. He stuffed away his wallet. "And we're a thousand dollars lighter!"

They tried eating at a restaurant, but the kids simply wouldn't settle down. So they headed back to the orphanage, once again in the dark.

They hadn't slept the previous night, and now they were faced with another sleepless night. It was too much. In the back seat of the can, Sharon's tears began to flow and she couldn't stop them. She was beyond exhausted.

Her tears turned to sobs, and suddenly Conor threw his arms around her. He hung on tight and didn't let go. Eventually he fell asleep like that.

"I needed that cry," she shared later. "It was like a refining fire from God."

But Rob knew her well.

Many hours later, after dropping off the kids at the orphanage, they got back to the hotel. Rob got out the Tylenol and gave Sharon a little sip of wine before gently tucking her into bed.

• • •

Her exhaustion lingered. A sore throat and touch of fever didn't help, nor did the fact that she unexpectedly ached with homesickness for her Canadian children. There was also the fact that in her vulnerable moments she was beating herself up for being incompetent and unworthy.

"Love is a choice, not a feeling," Rob told her. "Just like this whole project. We're doing it by faith, not by feelings."

Those words weren't just for Sharon; he needed them himself, not to mention some extra prayer time.

This was the lowest ebb in their journey. It scared them to think how close they got to throwing in the towel.

• • •

Their visits and long walks soon resumed. Their personal highs and lows came and went. That the kids were obviously intelligent and fast learners helped, as did their natural beauty.

One day, Rob's hearing aid batteries died and he couldn't find a place that sold them—that is, until one day they came upon a friendly man in a dark, dreadful alley in a dusty little shop. That's when they realized it was Christmas day. What a gift!

And so they spent the strangest Christmas ever in the strangest possible circumstances in a land they'd never been to and hoped never to see again.

Their smiles were right-side-up once more, and not without reason. The children had practiced hard and put on wonderful performances at the orphanage's Christmas concert. Niamh was a perfect angel.

Next came Conor's birthday, and then, on December 31, Declan turned six.

• • •

But soon their colds came back with a vengeance, as did a terrible toothache for Sharon. It got worse with pain that continued for days. What in the world? Her dental work had been up to date. Would all her teeth suddenly need to be pulled out? How could one possibly find a competent dentist in a situation like this?

An angel in disguise took them on an unprecedented journey that led to an old-fashioned dentist working out of a grubby office. The big woman's tools lay helter-skelter on a thoroughly chipped enamel tray. But this woman in the white coat knew exactly what she was doing and made the correct diagnosis: Sharon's previously cracked tooth had led to an abscess, which in turn had led to a massive sinus infection. This explained her relentless pain.

The dentist got out her pack of post-it notes and scribbled on them two prescriptions. Deeply appreciative, Rob got out his wallet, planning to pay her.

"Absolutely not," the woman said, vehemently.

"May I give you a hug then?" Sharon asked.

The woman nodded and the two embraced like long-lost friends.

The medication worked rapidly, much better than the eight-dollar price tag would have suggested.

And Sharon kept the post-it notes, a souvenir of God's remarkable faithfulness.

• • •

The paperwork was endless. Mistakes kept happening and the inevitable delays stretched on. A process that was to have lasted two or three weeks turned into eight.

However, the much-anticipated day finally arrived when they could live together as a family. Feeling ecstatic, everyone had huge smiles on their faces. Even the staff at the orphanage rejoiced.

The children's last day at the orphanage involved much more than joy. It involved eating and sleeping with their new parents without the aid of an interpreter. It also involved travelling to Kyiv for the final process of getting the kids' passports and visas—another potentially drawn-out waiting game.

Rob and Sharon needed to connect with their employers back in Canada, especially Rob's. The process was taking too long, and he kept hearing that his superiors were running out of patience. What could he do, though?

So far the whole venture had been such a remarkable God-thing, such an enormous answer to prayer. At times it had seemed almost unbelievable. Yet now a fresh reality stared them in the face: these kids had no idea how to do family. They behaved like calves out of a pen, with no concept of how to bond or show respect. Their very consciences were seared by lying, cheating, and selfishness.

For the first time, Rob and Sharon were overwhelmed by the task before them. Could they even do it? Were they in over their heads?

Thankfully, devotional readings helped. One that really tugged at Rob's heart spoke about godly endurance. He shared his reflections with Sharon.

"So what does that even look like?" he questioned. "Does that not mean clinging to God during the most difficult challenges? Does that not mean keeping our hope alive while holding tightly to His promises? Doesn't it involve a moment by moment posture of trust, knowing somehow that better things are coming, perhaps very soon?"

And then God performed a miracle.

• • •

Rob's employer had already given him one extension by this time, but how many more would they allow? Still, Rob and Sharon had to wait. They'd been told that the final stage of the adoption would take about a week. To kill time, they decided to look up some distant cousins of Rob's who apparently lived in Kyiv.

Wes and Kim Janzen weren't only members of an established evangelical church. Wes was also the director of the Kyiv Symphony Orchestra.

After making contact, Rob and Sharon were promptly invited over. Wes and Kim lived in a big, lovely house and were so warm in their hospitality. The whole visit was a godsend.

Wes listened well. When they heard of the latest delays, he stopped the couple.

"Hey," said Wes. "I can help. I have a friend, the Canadian ambassador here. He's a great guy and I'm pretty sure he would be happy to help you."

Really?

Well, he could and he would. This was their miracle. A process that should have taken at least a week managed to be concluded in just one day. Even the Ukrainian officials couldn't believe it. Like clockwork, the passports and visas showed up with a flourish.

• • •

The trip home was uneventful and the family arrived in time to save Rob's job—but only by the skin of his teeth, he was told.

It was now the middle of February 2017 and they'd reached the ugliest part of the greatest adventure of their lives—the making of a new family.

Every unrealistic expectation was cast aside in the days ahead as they came to understand that these kids were far more damaged than they'd realized. The years they'd spent in that orphanage had taught them many wrong things, but their pre-orphanage years had been even worse. They had suffered unimaginable abuse and neglect. Not only was all this abuse deeply embedded in their souls, but it somehow needed to find a way *out*. What better way could the children release the pain of their past than to throw temper tantrums? Or spit in Mama's face? Or run away and hide in a neighbour's cornfield for hours on end?

They did such things again and again.

Sharon's job gave her a parental leave of absence so she could be with the kids full-time. This involved taking care of many details, such as enrolling them in school and continually teaching, teaching, teaching—a new language, a new culture, a new life...

Would her patience pay off?

Rob and Sharon had carefully told the kids many lovely stories about Jesus, but one day, amidst all the hiccups, Niamh surprised them. She made a treasure hunt for her new parents using many slips of paper, each one containing a clue that led to the next place.

Finally the last slip of paper read "Niamh is now on Jesus's team."

Wow! Rob and Sharon hadn't seen this coming. They hugged her and gave her a hearty thumbs-up. Would this be the breakthrough they had been praying for?

It wasn't.

"Jesus," Sharon prayed one day in desperation. "Please show me. Is there anything I can do? What am I missing?"

In early June, an ad unexpectedly caught her attention. Someone was selling a mother hen with nine baby chicks. The quietest whisper vibrated in her heart: *You need to make a day trip out of this—with the kids, a crate for the chickens, and food for a picnic.*

When she checked with Rob on the phone about making this trip to the somewhat distant town of Carberry, he was as surprised as she.

This trip became a turning point. Was it the hours the four spent together? Was it the act of sharing such an old-fashioned adventure? Was it the process of figuring out which roads to take in order to arrive at this totally unknown place? Was it observing a mother hen and her chicks doing family so beautifully? Or was it simply God, saying that it was time?

Sharon had no answer. But this she knew: something changed that day. Yes, they would be a family. They would make it.

PART TWO
What More Do You Want of Us, Lord?
2019–2020

Rob couldn't believe it. Hadn't he just humbled himself and made a huge sacrifice for God and three of His neediest children? Hadn't he and Sharon done unusually much already, more than many would expect or consider normal?

Even Sharon seemed to disagree with him.

He could understand her, to some extent. She had left part of her heart in Ukraine. But so had he. That didn't mean they needed to go back and get more kiddos. Definitely not. The very idea was ludicrous. No way, absolutely no way, could such a nudging come from God.

No way.

The kids' prayers bothered him most. Every night they prayed together. The previous night, Conor had prayed, "And please make Daddy want to go back to Ukraine to adopt more of my friends."

Rob had sneaked a peek at Sharon. Had she put him up to that? No, she seemed as surprised as he.

All three of the kids had needed to hand in writing assignments at school talking about their adoption journey. Each of them, amidst their thankfulness, had included a line about hoping their new parents would go back to bring more kids out.

How could they even consider that? It was unthinkable.

The battle had been raging unabated for six long months and Rob was getting tired of it. He had become not only withdrawn but downright cranky.

Sharon wondered how long their marriage could survive, but she kept encouraging herself: *Hang on a little longer. Wait on the Lord. Even the strongest of saints have, throughout history, been known, sometimes in times of great stress or turmoil of the soul, to behave in uncharacteristic ways.*

And she had to give Rob that. His behaviour was definitely uncharacteristic.

• • •

Toward the end of Pastor Garry's sermon about God's sovereignty, Rob sensed Him pointing a finger toward him, saying, "Listen up." The pastor's question was simple: "Is He King of your life?"

Without warning, Rob saw himself in that question.

Is He King of my life?

And he didn't like the answer.

He had many valid reasons for not wanting to go back to Ukraine for more children. For one thing, solid Christian friends had advised him against it. Enough was enough. Some members of their family hadn't yet fully accepted the first three; whatever would they do with more?

Besides all this, their house wasn't ready. They had the square footage, but more bedrooms would have to be built and the space would have to be taken from his tool shed and storage area. He'd have to build a workshop outside, but there was no money left…

The list of objections went on and on, as it had for a long time now.

Something felt different today, though. Every point he made got a quick comeback, and those comebacks seemed to come from God Himself.

"You can make another loan and I will help you pay it back."

"But I haven't even paid back the loan from the first go around."

"That's okay. I am with you."

Then the text of Luke 14:26 flashed before his eyes. This wasn't a verse he had honed in on lately.

> If anyone comes to me and does not hate father and mother, wife and children, brothers and sisters—yes, even their own life—such a person cannot be my disciple.

Even while factoring in that this was meant as a comparison and that the word *hate* was symbolic, the words tore him apart. Suddenly the resistance inside him melted; he felt many pounds lighter as tears streamed down his face.

Now he just needed to have the courage to tell—no, to humbly admit—everything to Sharon. The call to go back for more kids wasn't her idea, nor was it Conor's or anyone else's. It was God's. Today he could finally see that.

• • •

A great battle had been won, but the war wasn't over. In his heart, Rob was committed to moving forward, but he also yearned for confirmation from his fellow believers. And he searched it out from his small group, from adult Sunday school participants, and from his pastor. Some of the feedback was incredibly supportive. Some sounded more like a warning.

Some of it was unique, too, like the guy who had come up to him with money in hand, wanting to support them.

But that man had posed a strange question: "If I support you now and this whole thing doesn't work out, could I get my money back?"

Rob had never considered that.

"Yeah," he finally replied. "I could go to the bank and make a loan to pay your part back, I imagine, if worse comes to worst."

And so his confusion continued to linger.

Until one day, in his morning Bible reading, he once more spread it all out before the Lord. In response, he saw the clearest possible picture of Jesus's bruised and bloodied body carrying the cross.

"Rob, each step I took was harder," He said. *"And not just because I knew what lay ahead, but because I was physically spent. But did I stop? No, I kept going... all the way... for you! Finally, I stumbled and fell and the guards had to get Simon of Cyrene to carry the timbers. Yet I got up again and followed. I went all the way for you, Rob. All the way."*

This encounter was profound, convicting, and motivating all at once. It moved him to believe Jesus had spoken to him. It suggested to Rob that the road ahead might be hard, and might get harder as they went forward.

But it also motivated him.

"Since Jesus kept going for me until His work was finished, no matter how horrific His road was, I want to keep going for Him too until my work is finished," he decided.

Human advice wouldn't have the final word.

• • •

Applying for and receiving the loan he needed to make the needed house renovations was only one of the steps that had to be taken by faith. He and Sharon also had to make appointments and applications regarding the adoption. By now they knew how to do it, but they didn't have the initial downpayment of $1,700.

Should they take out another loan? No. Should they write a series of post-dated cheques? No. Should they organize fundraisers? No. Should Sharon pick up extra shifts at work? No, she was already more than swamped.

On Wednesday, November 14, 2018, while working in his home office, Rob got an unexpected phone call from Sharon. It was two days before the big appointment in Winnipeg when the money needed to be in. He was deep in work mode and could hardly force himself to concentrate on what she was saying—at first.

"I just picked up the mail," she said for the third time.

He finally straightened up and listened.

"We just got a very unexpected cheque for $1,800," Sharon explained. "So we have the money for the application, plus the gas for driving in. We even have enough for a fish and chips dinner on the way home."

Wow! No wonder she was excited.

That cheque had come as a settlement from a company they had once upon a time invested in. The investment had been small and they had long since forgotten about it.

• • •

"How do your adopted kids feel about sharing their parents with more strangers?" several folks asked them. Rob didn't know how to answer. Apparently, many adopted kids guarded their new position jealously.

One night around the supper table he told all the kids about their new plan. Conor, who sat next to Rob, suddenly burst into tears. He put his head on his dad's shoulder and began to weep uncontrollably.

Rob and Sharon locked eyes, neither understanding their adopted son's reaction. Had they misread the situation? Did their adopted kids not want this after all?

Rob gently lifted Conor's tear-streaked face. "What's wrong, dear? Why aren't you happy about this? I thought you wanted…"

After several attempts, the boy was able to stop hiccupping long enough to speak coherently.

"Why did God choose *us* to be first when so many others are waiting?" Conor asked.

With that, Rob had the answer to his question. He couldn't answer Conor's, but he knew for himself that his kids were ready to go forward. His eyes moistened.

Reflecting back on this moment would be enough to propel him through many of the difficult days to come.

Sharon's conviction arrived during a special moment of connection with Niamh. Apparently someone had dared ask the girl how she felt about the prospect of another adoption, implying that it might cause her to lose the precious love of her new parents.

Niamh had been aghast at the very suggestion.

"Of course I know you won't stop loving me," she said to Sharon. "Haven't you proved it? Haven't you kept right on loving all your grown-up kids and their families even though we are here with you as your family now? Of course you'll keep on loving me."

Hearing those words moved her deeply.

• • •

Rob and Sharon soon shared their story in church. Afterward, two women came forward with an offer to spearhead the fundraising they would need. Several others, even strangers, volunteered to join them. Together, the group came up with fascinating ideas including garage sales, a pie auction, a painting night, building planters, and other fun events.

The group of fundraisers worked super hard in the days ahead. Even young kids set up a roadside stand in town and made a whopping $71.

All together, these efforts added up to $45,000. What a gift!

With this money in hand, Rob and Sharon only needed to take out a personal loan of $50,000, much less than they had thought.

Still, they both asked themselves turbulent questions. Did this really make sense for their family? But in the end, they agreed with the Bible: *"If God is for us, who can be against us?"* (Romans 8:31) God was calling them to this, and He would also see them through.

People absolutely thought they were crazy. One woman approached Sharon while having coffee and delivered a strange message.

"I feel led to tell you that this has to stop," the woman said. "You must stop adopting more kids. Instead go speak in various churches, and perhaps other settings, and teach other people how to adopt kids. You can't do it all. You shouldn't keep trying—"

"But that's not what God has called me to do," Sharon tried vainly to explain.

They were already acting according to God's calling.

"Everyone has three kinds of people backing them," Pastor Dylan later told them. "There are the cheerleaders, those who are quick to happily help out, pray, give, compliment, encourage. Then there are the naysayers, those who don't really understand but are eager to point out the risks and dangers lurking ahead. Finally, there are the mentors, those who are willing to go in the trenches with us through all the million steps a second adoption takes. They are the ones who offer shoulders to cry on and hold up our hands when we are broken and bleeding with discouragement. They challenge us and rebuke us and love us in spite of our faults… Surprisingly perhaps, we need each kind and I love them all. Each of the people in our lives fills a role and somehow fits into God's greater scheme, connecting us with His promise to be with us regardless—a promise He so often keeps by sending us just the right people at just the right time."

• • •

The in-between stages are always the hard ones, especially for those who are go-getters or have a tendency to feel restless. Rob and Sharon were no exception. They had lots of opportunities to practice their faith in the waiting.

Not that they had much quiet. Their renovations and gardening/canning projects, all done after working hours, kept them very occupied, as did all the preparatory work that needed to be done. They were thankful to see these things happen efficiently and smoothly, for the greater part. It was mouth-wateringly good. They could almost see the new kids coming home to their new rooms.

The one hitch revolved around waiting on legal paperwork to get done—paperwork that was absolutely essential but for some reason kept getting hijacked. From their end, Rob and Sharon had jumped through all the hoops correctly.

So why were these delays happening?

When a friend asked Rob about the delay, Rob explained the story in detail. Somehow, in the midst of his explanation, the whole situation crystallized for him and he unexpectedly saw it from a new angle.

"These seeming roadblocks are not roadblocks at all, but part of the Lord's doing," Rob realized aloud. "He's carefully laying out His plan for bringing our new children home."

At that moment, he felt Jesus put His arms around his shoulder and gently tell him, "I've got this. It's going to be okay."

As Rob shared this with his friend, they cried together for a while, both moved by the precious reality of God in their midst.

Rob was not prone to flights of fancy, so this was real.

That night, he and Sharon dusted off an old favourite verse:

> "For my thoughts are not your thoughts, neither are your ways my ways," declares the Lord. "As the heavens are higher than the earth, so are my ways higher than your ways and my thoughts than your thoughts." (Isaiah 55:8–9, NIV)

• • •

The question remained: how many kids would they bring home? While Rob had been in the so-called "war stage," he had argued, part in jest and part to prevent the whole thing from happening, that he would only go for more kids if they could adopt a family of eight siblings. Since that was highly unlikely and rather unrealistic, it sounded like a great deterrent.

That was before Rob submitted to God's will.

With his changed attitude, how would they decide the number? Rob was now willing to go for whatever number God had in mind for them.

Yet the more they prayed about it, the more Rob and Sharon felt that the number eight was actually meant to be their goal, despite the raised eyebrows they saw from people whenever they mentioned it.

At a meeting with adoption representatives from the provincial government, Rob and Sharon tentatively asked for up to eight siblings. This, of course, was met with shock.

"Can these people even do such a thing?" someone asked.

The dangling question silenced everyone in the room.

Oleg, their social worker, broke the stillness. "If anyone could manage it, these two could."

And since he knew Rob and Sharon so well by now, his word was accepted.

• • •

Unbelievable as it was, officials from the Ukrainian government confirmed that they actually did have a family of eight siblings waiting to be adopted. Rob and Sharon were told this despite the government's long-standing rule against adoptive parents being able to pick their children ahead of time. Rob and Sharon certainly didn't have any intention of breaking the rules.

One day, however, Sharon was forced to confront a heartbreaking struggle. What if those eight kids were all boys? Would she be able to handle them? She left the house crying that day, picturing eight strong and aggressive boys. The vision was so real that it overwhelmed her.

After some time, though, she was able to say, "It's okay, God. Whatever You have for us is fine. Whether it's boys, girls, or my preference—a nice mix. Whatever You choose."

She eventually returned home with a big smile on her tear-stained face.

But their plan to bring home these eight kids, even though they still had no idea who they were, met unexpected resistance.

It turned out that an American entrepreneur had already tried three times to adopt these same kids. Although he had fought vehemently, his bid for adoption had failed. Rob and Sharon didn't know all the details of what had happened, but they sensed clearly that the man's motives had been somehow off. They suspected that there may have been a very good reason that this person's quest had been repeatedly rejected.

When Rob and Sharon got back to Ukraine, they saw the files and were about to get the official go-ahead when they were abruptly stopped cold again. This time, a Ukrainian village priest had put in an application to adopt the same family.

What now, Lord? Sharon wondered.

The case was quite quickly and thoroughly analyzed. It turned out that though Ukrainians normally had first dibs, some of the details did not fall in this priest's favour. He wanted only to foster the kids, not adopt them. And he wanted them to work hard for him, for his own advantage, not theirs.

Thankfully, the right people saw through the request and turned it down. Soon Rob and Sharon were getting ready for another meeting with the adoption officials.

This time, everything went through.

• • •

It was déjà vu. After three years less a week, Rob and Sharon found themselves back in Kyiv—the very place they had once thought they'd never see again.

They landed safely in their apartment on November 24 at 4:30 p.m. It was located just a couple of blocks north of Independence Square. Very tired, but feeling safe and peaceful, they felt the prayers of friends following them.

They also heard still the voice of Pastor Dylan, who had reminded them of Joshua 1:9:

Have I not commanded you? Be strong and courageous. Do not be frightened, and do not be dismayed, for the Lord your God is with you wherever you go. (ESV)

Rob pondered this verse a lot during the current adoption stage.

Courage is a mark of faith in the Lord, he told himself. *The Lord does not want us to shrink back or cower in the face of adversity or trial. Rather, He expects that we will face it boldly, head on—not in our own strength, but in His.*

"Thank You, Jesus, for making a way," Sharon wrote in her journal at night. "Thank You, Jesus, for all who stand by our side in prayerful support!"

• • •

"Why would you bother coming for these children?" a worker carefully asked them one day. "Don't you know that these kids are ignorant, stupid, lazy, and whatnot? Why would you even bother?"

What a depressing question. Rob and Sharon had no answer for this man.

Thankfully, of the eight workers they dealt with, this was the only one with such a dark mindset. The other seven were very supportive and quite appreciative of their efforts. These people felt like friends working toward the same goal.

• • •

Soon they were ready to meet the kids for the first time. The siblings weren't coming from one orphanage, but rather from three different facilities.

Were Rob and Sharon really ready to take this step?

Just like last time, it was to be a momentous day filled first with eager anticipation and then the excitement of their new reality.

But only seven children were brought in to meet them. Who was missing?

For reasons unknown to Rob and Sharon, the youngest, Patrick, had not yet been introduced to them.

Other than that, everything went smoothly. Their hotel room was the same as last time, as was the three-kilometre walk back and forth for each visit, often twice a day. During these walks, and sometimes stops in coffee shops, they were surprised by the affection they received from strangers. These people even remembered them, some by name. Some actually hugged them like long-lost friends. How cool was that?

• • •

One aspect of this trip, though, was very different. They had the opportunity to become friends with several people from a local evangelical church, including Pastor Valentine and Slavic and others. This connection came about through their new friends, Mike and Trish, who had been to Ukraine recently, also on an adoption journey.

Where had this church been on their first trip to Ukraine? Was it really so small that hardly anyone had known about it? Because three years ago they had asked and searched for a local evangelical church but found nothing.

These people became a rock for them. Not only did Rob and Sharon now have a church to connect with and attend, but they also developed close friendships. They had people to relax, laugh, and shoot the breeze with, people who loved to pray for them and with them. These people took a personal interest in their story and delighted in praying for each one of their new kiddos, even and maybe especially for the still missing one—little Patrick.

There was no way to measure the worth of such a blessing.

• • •

"The day they brought Patrick to spend time with us opened our eyes, at least partway, to the possibility of deep-seated health issues," Sharon wrote in her journal. "Nobody said anything. They didn't need to. This five-year-old was obviously out-of-control hyperactive. The way he kept jumping under things and over people and all was crazy. Rob and I locked eyes and somehow knew. We are, after all, healthcare workers."

And yet all eight of these children had passed the required medical check to make them eligible for adoption. Each had the approved health certificate to prove it.

Despite the apparent problems, both Rob and Sharon fell in love with Patrick. Little did they know, however, just how much more was to come.

• • •

Once again the days turned into weeks, and the weeks into months. The COVID-19 pandemic was wreaking havoc everywhere. They saw the results on the streets of the cities they visited as store after store closed their doors.

They felt the severity of the situation more acutely in Kyiv as they kept waiting for the final adoption papers to arrive. Practicing patience was one thing, but the matter was becoming downright urgent. They had to get home before all flights would be cancelled and restrictions tightened further.

"God, what's happening?" Sharon prayed. "Are You in this?"

Still missing some passports and ID cards for the kids, Rob and Sharon arranged a consult with the Canadian ambassador. He finally gave them a temporary pass of sorts for the kids who still needed one. He signed a simple piece of paper with the photos and data pertaining to the three oldest girls.

Really? Would that suffice? Would that see them through all three international airports?

Unbelievably, it did.

And yes, God was in it. At each leg of the journey, they heard the same grim reminders: "This is the last flight out" or "This is Canada's final effort to bring all its people home."

The final outcome was amazing. In Toronto, they beat the new quarantine rules by just thirty minutes. Had they come in any later, they would have had to isolate in a hotel for two weeks before continuing home.

After arriving home, they still had to isolate for five weeks, but at least they were home and together with their other three kiddos.

It may have helped that soon after their return, someone organized a welcome-to-Canada parade of cars, about sixty in total, to drive slowly by their place as all thirteen members of the family came to the end of their driveway to watch. Each car passed with banners, balloons, or ribbons flying, accompanied by hearty shouts of joy.

As always, God showed up at just the right moments and in just the right ways, revealing His will one step at a time. And the praise was all His.

PART THREE

As the Saga Unfolds

2020

Rob and Sharon arrived home with their eight new kids on March 20, 2020, smack in the middle of COVID with all its fears and restrictions. They isolated for five weeks, all the while dealing with their misgivings about the children's actual health stories. Although they had all gotten doctor-signed medical approvals in Ukraine, some things didn't feel right.

Without knowing why, Sharon felt a great urgency to learn the truth, and to do it in a hurry. Their new daughter Meara seemed to have a heart issue, and Patrick obviously had ADHD. But she was convinced there was more to discover.

Although ten-year-old Fallon was happy, intelligent, and had the widest, most beautiful smile, something seemed amiss. Her skin had a sallow look, her appetite was horrible, and she was seriously small and underweight for her age. What was going on?

Sharon had noticed an unpleasant odour coming from the girl's skin. It made her think of rotting fish. Maybe they would need a deeper, better bathtub?

But nothing helped and the situation didn't improve.

Sharon scheduled appointments with their family doctor, who was also a friend, immediately after the isolation order lifted. When the day came for all the children to get their checkups, everything went smoothly enough—as smoothly as such things can go when eight children are involved. The bloodwork and tests were done.

Nothing could have prepared Sharon for the urgent phone call they received the very next day from the doctor himself.

"There are a number of issues going on with your kids," he said. "Most of those can wait. There will be time to discuss them soon enough. But there is one…"

He heaved a big sigh and paused for a moment. Sharon wondered if she needed to sit down. Something about his tone scared her.

"Um… Fallon is in acute end-stage kidney failure. If we hope to save her, you must take her to the emergency room immediately at Health Sciences Centre's Children's

Hospital in Winnipeg. You have no time to lose. I've made all the arrangements…"

"What?" Sharon did need to sit down. She wasn't just imagining this. "What's going on?"

When he told her the facts, she understood his words all too readily, being a nurse herself.

"Her creatinine is at 1169," he explained.

Creatinine is a type of protein excreted through a person's urine. A normal creatinine number should fall between 60 to 110, but hers was ten times the upper limit. And allowing for her age and small stature, her personal normal should have been between 40 and 80.

Sharon wasn't sure how many minutes she sat there in shock. Hadn't they just celebrated Fallon's eleventh birthday while still hoping blindly that all was well?

Probably she only sat there for a matter of seconds. But what happened next she remembered much better: the burst of action that followed.

Instead of succumbing to panic and fear, instead of running around in circles or screaming demands, Sharon demonstrated nerves of steel.

"I cry as much as anybody does," she would later say. "I get flustered and frustrated like all humans do."

But on this particular day, her nerves of steel sprung forth like the flowers in her garden.

Who would take Fallon to Winnipeg, and who would stay with her for everything that was sure to follow? Who would take care of the other ten kiddoes? Who would deal with meal prep and the hundred and one things that needed to be done in their bustling household?

• • •

In May 2020, Rob drove Fallon to the hospital in Winnipeg.

"I stayed behind to pack, sort out some meals, and get someone to mind the kids until Rob could come back," Sharon said later. "Our hastily assembled plan was for me to stay with Fallon at the Health Sciences Centre Children's Hospital for as long as it would take. I needed to be prepared. This was eighty-eight kilometres away from our home, so I couldn't expect to run back and forth easily for forgotten items."

Her friend Carrie was happy to take her to the Children's Hospital that very afternoon. When she arrived, Fallon had just had an arterial line put in to give her medications to lower her blood pressure and also monitor it. Her blood pressure was dangerously high, 182/129, and the doctors were afraid she could have a stroke.

In the beginning, and for quite some time to follow, her blood pressure didn't respond to any medications, not even the ones administered by IV.

As hard as it was to believe, Fallon truly was in end-stage renal failure. And as far as anyone could see, there was little hope. Very little appeared to be going in the girl's favour.

Yet Rob and Sharon were heart-and-soul agreed that as long as there was life, there was hope. And there was God! He had brought the family through every obstacle so far, so why would He desert them now? Surely He had a plan. They would lean hard into Him, step by step, and trust Him to show up for whatever was ahead.

Very soon, hundreds of people were praying, organized by various prayer teams. Not only did this reassure Rob and Sharon, but it was also quite literally life-giving. When their minds and bodies were too exhausted to form proper prayers, they counted on the Spirit to intercede for them with groans that cannot be uttered (Romans 8:26–27). They also counted on praying friends to pick up the slack.

Through it all, the bottom line was unchangeable: Fallon was like a flesh-and-blood daughter. They loved her with a passion and were prepared to spare no effort in the fight for her life. Whatever it would take, Lord willing, they would give.

• • •

They soon developed a routine. Sharon stayed with Fallon while Rob managed the homefront, kept up his job, and drove in almost every evening for a brief visit at the hospital. Fallon adored him and really looked forward to these visits.

Rob also arranged for caregivers in his absence. COVID-19 kept wreaking havoc with this routine, but he gallantly made it work.

Since two parents weren't allowed to visit at the same time, he and Sharon had to take turns. During Rob's visit, Sharon would go outside for a walk. All the places to sit down were closed or forbidden at this time, but she found one bench that wasn't. It turned out to be a good stopping point.

After a while, Rob started bringing one or two of the kids with him for these evening visits. One day, Conor came and snuggled up beside Sharon on the bench. He put his head on her lap and fell soundly asleep before either knew what was happening. Oh, how he had missed his mama!

When it was Patrick and Meara's turn, they sat outside with Sharon and began to look for bugs, just to entertain themselves. They made a contest out of seeing who could find the most bugs and figure out how many kinds there were. They eagerly showed off each one to Sharon.

"Good thing I wasn't one of those queasy mammas who nearly faint at the sight of creepy crawlies, right?" she murmured.

• • •

Many people helped at the homefront. Some folks delivered meals. Others brought snacks and treats. Still others stayed with the kids or stopped in often just because they cared. Occasionally, people sent money to help meet the family's expenses.

No matter what shape or size these love packages came in, each was appreciated.

• • •

Fallon's journey remained tough. When it wasn't one thing, it was another. It seemed that every time one crisis was resolved, another popped up. This continued day after day, week after week, until during her fifth week in the paediatric ICU. Only then did the doctors feel she was stable enough to try moving her to the regular ward.

She was only in the regular ward for two days before once again all hell broke loose. She contracted sepsis from an infection in the haemodialysis line in her neck. Sharon knew only too well the danger of sepsis. It was a deadly killer as often as not, and something to drive staff to run, not walk, to their next step of duty.

In the middle of the night, a doctor rapidly pushed her bed down the halls back to the PICU. No one expected her to live, they later admitted, but they fought for her life with everything they had at their disposal.

Between these efforts and God's infinite wisdom, something worked, praise the Lord. Sharon and Rob were thankful beyond words.

• • •

The area of Winnipeg where Sharon went walking during Rob's visit probably wasn't the safest place to go alone, she admitted later.

"I did meet some interesting people, but I knew I was protected. Instead of dwelling on fear, I tried to hone in on being thankful. I couldn't help but be thankful! I marvelled at the fact that God doesn't make mistakes. He knew that Fallon was sick when no one else did. He knew that her kidneys hadn't grown since she was a baby, that they were badly scarred and the size of grapes."

Yes, God was fully aware that they were going to come to the rescue. Sharon marvelled at the awesome goodness of such a Father who loved Fallon so very much. It was a miracle in itself that she had survived long enough to be adopted.

"It just blows me away!" she said. "He also knew she would need two nurses for parents."

But her journey wasn't over. In fact, it had only just begun.

• • •

Fallon endured the pain of many surgeries: to install a haemodialysis line in her neck, to put a peritoneal dialysis catheter in her abdomen, a PICC line in her arm, and an arterial line in her wrist. She suffered constant emesis and retched every single time she went for her daily haemodialysis—that is, until two weeks had passed, allowing her to begin peritoneal dialysis.

All these struggles helped her bond tightly to Sharon, her frontline caregiver. She needed to be lifted out of bed to use the commode, not to mention a host of other tasks.

During this time, Fallon became totally fluent in English, so much so that when someone in the hospital tried to speak Russian to her, she pretended she didn't understand it, even though of course she did.

Through every ordeal, Fallon remained amazingly cheerful. Her wide smiles, sparkling eyes, and sweetly optimistic attitude endeared her to everyone around her, including doctors and caregivers of every kind.

Yet sometimes even an incredible attitude isn't enough.

When the staff eventually started the daily peritoneal dialysis, the drain pain was so bad that Fallon would cry and whimper through the night. It was exhausting for both her and Sharon. Every forty-five minutes at night, the cycle would drain and she'd cry in pain. Warm blankets helped a little, but sometimes Sharon had to crawl into bed and hold her tightly. What else could she do?

Through all the twists and turns, Fallon got very attached to her beloved stuffed brown bear. How she found room for him was a mystery, though, amidst all those tangles of tubes and gadgets. Yet room she found, always. She never considered that a problem.

• • •

One day, Auntie Alyson bought Fallon a blue T-shirt that had the word Waymaker printed on the front with a bright yellow sunflower. She also brought a huge banner that read "Get Well Soon Fallon," signed by friends and well-wishers with lots of messages of support and encouragement.

Along with many other tangible gifts, including meals that just kept coming, this gesture provided another visible reminder of the care she was receiving.

This is what the hands and feet of Jesus look like: love in action!

• • •

On the homefront, the drama never stopped.

Meara, who had by now been diagnosed with a heart murmur, was told she needed to have the aortic valve in her heart replaced. But the doctors were concerned, since she was so small and skinny. Surgery would have a much higher chance of success if she could grow a little bigger and stronger.

So began a new routine. Every three months, Meara visited the Variety Heart Clinic in Winnipeg for tests. They hoped to keep this up until she was a teenager. So far, her progress seemed promising.

Then, in July, Patrick spiked a high fever and ended up being rushed to the emergency room to have his appendix removed. During his hospital stay, he also tested positive for Lyme disease. It had already been a full-time job taking care of his earlier diagnoses of ADHD, microcephaly, and global developmental delay—or at least that's what it felt like, especially after she went back to work four days a week as a diabetes educator.

Still, she was eternally thankful for this adorable little boy who had so blessed their family. They couldn't turn their back on him for a second, though, or he would get into something he wasn't meant to get into.

On their country driveway, from where they meet the bus going to and from school.

Family supper on any given day.

Driving places (church, family outings) in their super-sized van.

• • •

"And so our life continues, good days and then some not so good ones," Sharon posted one day on social media. "But now that we're in it a way, I think we have more good days. Just don't ask me that question in the middle of a bad one or I may be tempted to say something I would regret. The truth is it's hard to learn to live with so many people with so many different personalities, strong wills, trauma issues, and medical conditions and not be negatively affected by it all. It's also the time-consuming and bone-draining effort of pouring into lives, often getting nothing back for a long time, if ever. I'm working on releasing such disappointments to God since I know I cannot carry them on my own shoulders. That is the only way, I believe, I can live in freedom—the kind of freedom Jesus offers His followers."

Never would she and Rob have imagined what it would really mean to claim for themselves the words of Isaiah:

> But now thus says the Lord, he who created you, O Jacob, he who formed you, O Israel: "Fear not, for I have redeemed you; I have called you by name, you are mine. When you pass through the waters, I will be with you; and through the rivers,

they shall not overwhelm you; when you
walk through fire you shall not be burned,
and the flame shall not consume you. For
I am the Lord your God, the Holy One of
Israel, your Savior." (Isaiah 43:1–3, ESV)

But that's how it had been. They had never needed
Him more—and they had never before seen such a
dazzling display of His power come through when they
needed it most.

"The cost of this adoption has been much more than
just financial," she wrote. "Yes, the financial part is huge.
Despite all the gifts, it may take us a lifetime to finish
paying off the debt. The giving up of personal freedoms to
relax and indulge could be cited as one thing. Sometimes
our energy runs out before we can love on all our older
kids properly, or on the adorable little grands, too, which
we do try to keep up with."

An even bigger sacrifice was the question of whether
she would ever be able to travel to Ireland to visit her
mother, who was ill, and leave Rob alone with the whole
gang. Disregarding the financial cost of such a trip, she
didn't know how she could possibly leave him to look after
eleven children while also managing work and being there
for Fallon for dialysis ten hours every night. That didn't

even account for the full stream of emotional issues the family had to deal with every day.

When Fallon did finally come home, she had to take twenty-three pills daily and get a weekly injection to help her body make red blood cells. Later they added a tube feed to help her get enough protein, since her poor appetite wasn't cutting it. She needed to gain size and strength to prepare her for a kidney transplant. Hopefully one day.

"This journey is something we went into with our eyes open," Sharon said. "As far as it was humanly possible, details notwithstanding, we desired to be obedient to God. But if we're honest, we do grieve from time to time. That's not complaining, just stating the fact. This is the reality of our lives."

Although Sharon couldn't make the trip to Ireland, she felt incredibly thankful for having had the opportunity earlier to say goodbye to her mother while on a three-day stopover. She and Rob had gone there on their way to Ukraine for the second adoption.

"We made some beautiful memories and those few hours I got to spend with her are something I will always treasure," she said. "I think we both said goodbye many times in those few hours! Her dependence on Jesus and thankfulness in all situations has left me with an incredible example to follow."

PART FOUR

Love Can Be Costly

2023

Life has a way of moving onward. The clock doesn't stop ticking, no matter what one's issues are. So let's fast-forward some two and a half years.

Fallon's dialysis wasn't cutting it anymore, not even when the doctors upped it to twelve hours per night. She was already sacrificing most of her social time with her siblings, hooked up to all those machines. She would hear them play in the distance while she lay alone upstairs.

They'd all been praying and hoping for a kidney transplant one day. Would that day ever come? Was it even realistic to keep hoping? The signs weren't good. Yes, she had gained the necessary weight and stature, but the doctors seemed to be running out of options while they waited. Her vitals were getting worse instead of better.

Simply put, she wasn't doing well—not at all. Were they going to lose the battle?

• • •

"There must be something more we can do," Sharon said aloud while brainstorming one night with Rob. "Surely God didn't bring us this far for nothing. Surely the promise in Jeremiah 29:11 applies to her, to us, in this situation."

> "For I know the plans I have for you," declares the Lord, "plans to prosper you and not to harm you, plans to give you hope and a future."

That's when it struck her: they would tell her story in the media—on the radio, on TV, in newspapers, wherever they could find an in. And they would include a desperate appeal each time: "Time is running out. She needs a transplant *now*."

And they would ask their many prayer partners to pray—to pray like they'd perhaps never prayed before.

• • •

They received a lot of responses. Emotional calls. Financial gifts. A promised increase of prayer support. But beyond that? Nothing.

They decided to repeat the process.

And then again.

"God, where are You?" they cried in desperation. "When will the answer come?"

They clung to hope, hanging on to God's promises, all the while reminding themselves to *"be still, and know that I am God"* (Psalm 46:10). This verse had so often been a sermon to them. They often saw it as a description of God's waiting room, a place where one can be glad because God is good and be still because He is active whether or not one can see it.

They kept on waiting, month after month, and hoping against hope. And they prayed—hard.

Until one day everything changed.

• • •

For three years, almost to the day, Fallon had been on a very intensive dialysis regime, with hope dwindling and no end in sight. On a chilly spring day in mid-April 2023, the telephone buzzed around midnight.

"We think we have a match," the voice on the other end of the line informed Rob. "If all goes well, we have a kidney for Fallon."

Although everything didn't change in one fell swoop, as would have been so wonderful, that call did introduce them to the most exciting and exhilarating week in their history as a family.

The preparations began immediately.

Despite the excitement, of course, there was also another side of the story. When someone hears that a child's kidney is available for donation, they must realize that another family somewhere is likely grieving a precious child and trying gallantly to bring something good out of their tragic loss.

The family realized that their hope and rejoicing came at a great and unwanted expense, lending great sombreness to an already heart-rending day.

Soon Fallon was being hooked up and prepped for the complicated surgery. She waited in her room, anticipating the moment when she would be wheeled into the OR. Both Sharon and Rob sat with her.

Without warning, the process seemed to stall. Although the match had been designated as good, a few things were going wrong. Perhaps it had something to do with the fever and pneumonia the donor had suffered in the end, but a last-minute final check revealed that the transplant wouldn't be successful.

The whole plan had to be aborted.

The doctor herself was in tears when she told them. Everyone was so disappointed and worried. In fact, the doctor had been quite certain that Rob and Sharon would be angry. But their calm response surprised her.

"It's okay," Rob said. "We're not blaming anyone. It must not have been the right time yet. If God is sovereign—and we really believe He is—we are totally okay with this. He has a better plan in mind…"

Back home they went, back to the grind, back to the twelve-hour dialysis every day… back to waiting.

Somehow, strangely, they had peace. It felt to them as if God was sitting right there in the waiting room with them.

• • •

Some ten days later, the phone buzzed again. The same excited tone, but a different voice; the same message, but a different doctor.

At first Sharon wondered whether this was an accidental replay of the former call. Was this somebody's crazy idea of a prank? It was still April, after all.

Despite the temptation, though, she didn't hang up. She couldn't. Pinching herself to make sure she wasn't sleep-walking, she tentatively asked the person on the phone to repeat the message.

Even hearing it a second time didn't totally convince her. Her disbelief came through loud and clear.

"You mean to tell me that after three years of hearing nothing, we get two calls within little more than a week?"

"Yes," the doctor replied. "We have a kidney for Fallon. If you can bring her in right away…"

Truly?

Sharon had a strong impulse to laugh. This had to be one of the strangest developments ever.

• • •

A shroud seemed to hover over the family, as though they were all in a daze while they once again readied themselves for surgery. They managed to get to the city in record time, safe and sound, ready to once more begin the complicated preparation.

What would come next?

This time, there were no holdups. No hiccups even. Everything seemed to be on track, nicely following the script in some doctor's textbook.

First, of course, there was the usual waiting. They were ready to go but didn't know for sure when everything would begin. Would this be another case of expectations gone awry, like with premature labour? Or would this finally be the day everything worked?

• • •

APRIL 28

The last hour of waiting felt like forever. It was crunch time and everyone had gotten up early. The list of required tests for Fallon had seemed endless. She'd done bloodwork, given a urine sample, gotten hooked up to an IV, and done peritoneal dialysis, to name a few.

Then the nephrologist came to see them to outline the plan. The donor would be taken into the OR at 2:00 p.m., and by three o'clock they would know whether the kidney was viable.

Every breath, every moment, in the waiting was a unique ache in the chest, yet it was combined with that special kind of peace that comes from God alone.

> "For my thoughts are not your thoughts,
> neither are your ways my ways," declares
> the Lord. (Isaiah 55:8)

Submitting to this truth was so vital, even though it was also a challenge. Hadn't Rob prayed faithfully for a transplant before Fallon's next birthday? Would God make that happen?

The eternal God is your refuge, and underneath are the everlasting arms. (Deuteronomy 33:27)

And then the answer came.

"It's a go," the doctor told them.

Fallon was rolled into the OR quickly, but not before the surgeon who'd perform the transplant met Rob and Sharon. When they told him that they were praying for him and all the doctors involved, he put his arms around Rob appreciatively and said softly, "I'm a dad, too. I get this."

Fallon went into surgery at 5:10 p.m. Just before she left, Rob suggested that she name her new kidney. She decided on Quinn, after her best friend.

They watched "Quinn," the new kidney, get placed in a blue cooler and regretted not having remembered to snap a picture.

Just like that, they went back into waiting mode, this time with great expectancy.

"We are eternally grateful to the donor and their family for this amazing gift," Sharon wrote during this time.

The waiting game had only just begun.

When Fallon came out of surgery, the family learned that the procedure had gone well. She was taken to PICU and her blood pressure was very low. They would have to keep giving her IV meds to bring it up. In fact, there were about ten infusions running at this time, some short-term and others continuous.

She was very tired, understandably so, but woke up once to squeeze Rob's hand. Another time she asked Sharon to wash her eyes before immediately falling asleep again.

The big thing to watch and wait for was whether "Quinn" would start producing urine. That was the crucial test, and so far there was nothing.

APRIL 29

Fallon had a reasonable night. Although her face was very puffy, she was alert and had already told someone that she was bored.

The pain medications were doing their job—and now the big issue was for "Quinn" to wake up and start doing her job. So far there had been a tiny trickle of urine, but it wasn't nearly enough. They were looking for a minimum of thirty millilitres per hour.

Nine infusions were currently running now.

For some reason, the song "The Battle Belongs to You, O Lord" played over and over in both of Rob and Sharon's brains that day. They kept encouraging each other with the thoughts expressed in it.

"We do our best fighting on our knees," one would say to the other. "With God, all things are possible."

Rob had stayed home for a while to get needed things done, but he returned as soon as he could. By evening, Fallon was asking him to watch a movie with her. This was beautiful to see. Despite her swollen face, she was getting back to her positive self.

Just before Rob got up to leave for the night, the happy nurse almost squealed with excitement.

"We've got it. We've got it!"

She'd just measured—there were forty millilitres of urine. It had been slow in coming—scarily slow, unexpectedly slow, since they already look for that result in the operating room—but the moment had arrived.

Why it took more than twenty-four hours, nobody knows. What they do know is that it did finally happen. To all concerned, it seemed like a miracle.

APRIL 30

When Sharon arrived in the morning, she was greeted by the doctors. They were gravely concerned, because Fallon's haemoglobin had dropped to 64 overnight. It had been 94 the previous day. They suspected an internal bleed, since there was a lot of pain and pressure in Fallon's abdomen.

The staff was arranging for an ultrasound to confirm this while also prepping her for a blood transfusion. She was very hot and pale.

While Sharon was formulating the words to ask for more prayer support, the nurse dashed up to her excitedly.

"The blood just arrived for her," the nurse said. "Never in my life have I seen it come this fast."

So God was with them even amidst the drama.

Yet Fallon didn't seem to worry. She was so brave, despite being life-threateningly sick. As the girl moaned in pain, Sharon called Rob; he would come as soon as he was able.

By 10:18, Fallon was being taken in for emergency surgery to stop the bleeding. They would also place a dialysis line in her neck, as well as a PICC line in her arm, so they would have quick access whenever and wherever they might need it.

As the wait began all over again, Sharon was struck anew by a powerful realization: *Fallon is a child of God. Regardless of how all this goes, He's got her.*

While Sharon sat in the waiting room, the text of Romans 8:38 flashed through her brain. She hadn't brought her Bible and couldn't verify the exact wording, but she was pretty sure she got the gist of it right.

> For I am convinced that neither death nor life, neither angels nor demons, neither the present nor the future, nor any powers, neither height nor depth, nor anything else in all creation, will be able to separate us from the love of God that is in Christ Jesus our Lord.

That promise strengthened her like nothing else could have.

In the midst of these profound thoughts Sharon felt motivated to write a bit of a tribute for Fallon.

> If I could choose one word to describe Fallon, it would be *joyful*. From the time we met her the first time at the orphanage in Ukraine, she has always had a smile on her face. When we were there for our first adoption in 2016—for Niamh, Conor, and Declan—she, just a tiny little thing with black shining eyes and a giant smile, came rushing out to meet us at the gate.

It didn't matter that we weren't there for her; she was joyful for her friends. She'd be among the first to see us and would come feet flying, throw her arms around Rob's legs in the tightest of hugs, and then joyfully run off again.

Three years later when we were back for her and her siblings, she had not forgotten us any more than we her. In spite of the fact that, unknown to anyone, she was in end-stage kidney failure, and obviously not feeling well, she was still smiling. Constantly.

When we were home with her for only five weeks, in the middle of COVID, we got the devastating news of her condition. We spent five and a half weeks right here, just one room down the hall, fighting for her life. I remember almost losing her through sepsis, setting up the dialysis, and so much more… Through all of that, she remained joyful…

Sharon needed to get back to the moment at hand, for Fallon had gotten back from surgery. The doctors had removed a haematoma, a large blood clot, in the pole of her kidney and then sealed off the bleeder.

The good news was that Fallon now had her dialysis and PICC lines. The doctor had also been able to recycle some of her own blood and give it back to her in the OR.

While still waiting for Rob, a nurse who had worked with them three years ago remembered Sharon and came to give her a hug. God is so good!

MAY 1

Fallon had a poor night, with lots of pain despite the patient-controlled fentanyl pump. She had developed a fever and her haemoglobin had dropped again, this time to 61, despite the previous day's blood transfusion.

When Sharon walked in, she saw Fallon receiving a blood transfusion of irradiated packed red cells—the same kind given to cancer patients—and haemodialysis simultaneously. Her creatinine was 1503.

"Today the toll of the last 72 long hours is really showing on her tiny body and mind," Sharon wrote. "She is very flat. For one of the first times ever, the sparkle of joy is not there. We had tried to warn her, but what's happening is so much more than anybody could have known."

The school principal called Sharon to say that the whole school was praying and standing with Fallon. They were trying to support her siblings as needed. What a blessing!

Then a friend sent her a song: "Endless Praise," by Charity Gayle. She and Fallon listened together, and then listened again. It helped.

MAY 2

Fallon had been moved out of the PICU to the regular ward around 5:00 p.m. the previous night. She had dialysis in the morning, followed by some other tests, all of which went well.

There had been only one blip. In the afternoon, her blood pressure suddenly shot up again and she needed IV meds to bring it back into the target range.

The good news was that "Quinn" continued to produce urine. Both Rob and Sharon remarked that they had never before been so excited to see someone pee!

They both agreed that Jesus was answering their prayers of faith, since without faith it is impossible to please God. They had been asking for big things and receiving even bigger answers.

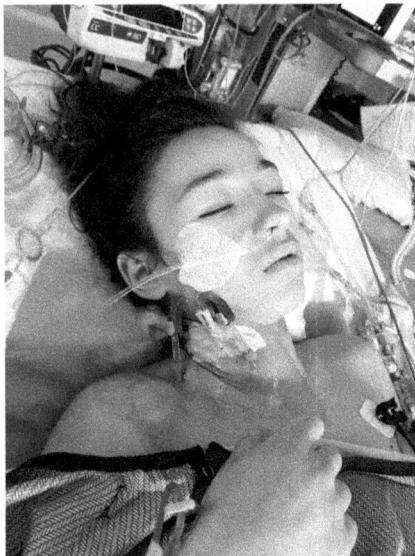

Fallon, when the hope for her life was very low.

Rob and Sharon visiting Fallon.

Fallon, on a better day, with her beloved bear.

MAY 3

Fallon had a good night. There was much reason to be thankful, and that morning she went through dialysis on the third floor.

There was a new concern, though. Although "Quinn" was producing urine, it still wasn't at a healthy level.

While this wasn't what anyone desired, it wasn't totally unexpected. There's a name for this: delayed graft function. It happens most often when the donor has already been deceased.

Now Rob and Sharon put forward a new prayer request, for "Quinn" to graft so well into Fallon's body that it would be almost impossible to tell the difference from a normal kidney.

Sharon got a surprise invite out for coffee from friends. This proved to be her first time leaving the hospital since the latest drama had begun.

"Thank You, Jesus, for laughter and for hugs," Sharon wrote that night.

MAY 4

Fallon ate a banana this day, which probably doesn't sound too exciting. But it was! She loved bananas but hadn't been able to eat one for three years because her potassium had been too high.

Her infectious joy continued to surprise everyone around the ward. Yet when a visitor wanted to bless her with a song and asked for a favourite, Fallon surprised them all with her choice: "You Say," by Laura Daigle. The song reflected a Christian's innate struggle with feeling that they aren't enough, that they're too weak and don't belong.

The song also reminds us so beautifully that Jesus tells us the very opposite. His loving affirmation overrules all that negativity. What we need to do is believe.

Later in the day, Sharon left for a little bit while Rob stayed. Fallon always loved her dad time.

At home, Sharon could finally have a proper bath and find a new batch of clean clothes. But the big push was to attend the local school's production of *Charlie and the Chocolate Factory*. Three of their older girls were starring in it and Sharon knew her presence would mean a lot to them. She wouldn't have left Fallon if the girl had still been in trouble—the memories of almost losing her daughter were too fresh in her mind—but now that things seemed to be going better, she decided to give herself a treat: to laugh and enjoy herself with family and friends.

MAY 8

Fallon's best friend Quinn, the real live Quinn, came to visit her at the hospital. The two had already been best friends in Ukraine, and then Quinn had been adopted by another family in the area, allowing the girls to again pursue their friendship.

When Quinn arrived, she promptly crawled into bed with Fallon. Even the required masks couldn't hide their huge smiles or cover up their giggles.

MAY 10

It was Fallon's birthday and she turned fourteen. Rob's prayer, that she would get her kidney before her next birthday, had been answered with a resounding yes.

In honour of her birthday, she received a video clip from Ukraine, from the very friends Rob and Sharon had made while there. This supportive friendship had now been ongoing, such a precious reminder of the amazing goodness of God.

They were starting to see better urine production from "Quinn," since Fallon's creatinine had climbed to 290. It wasn't perfect, but it was such a vast improvement.

MAY 13

What a day! The family rejoiced as Fallon was discharged from the hospital. They would still be required to make daily trips to Winnipeg for blood draws, which would be a challenge, but all in all they had so much to be thankful for.

Even at home, Fallon would need to stay in isolation for three months. While that might feel long, they knew that they would get through it.

MAY 22

It had been over a week since Fallon's return home and she had steadily improved each day. However, one of the biggest challenges was her medication regimen.

"It almost scared the pants off me," Sharon later said. "Counting out meds all day? There were so many new ones in addition to the ones she was already on. And the price tags! The anti-rejection drugs alone cost over $1,900 per month, which we paid for out of pocket until pharmacare kicked in. And you know how that goes—those numbers are calculated on income. Since Rob and I both worked, this would take several months. If it weren't for the repertoire we already had under our belts, about God's amazing faithfulness, the very thought of all this wouldn't only frighten me; it would paralyze me."

• • •

"Our life as a family is about more than Fallon's story," Sharon said. "She is, after all, only one of the eleven children we're raising. We have spent an impossible amount of time, energy, and money on her for years now. But that doesn't mean we love the others less."

People sometimes asked them the strangest questions. For example, "If you had known all this was going to happen, would you still have adopted these kiddos?"

"Of course, we would have," she adamantly said. "And if we should discover a million more problems, we would never want to reverse that decision. Never ever."

That being said, it sure wasn't easy. They sometimes struggled, thinking about how hard adoption could be. But then they'd get an unexpected boost, such as this note Rob got from Meara one day: "I love you dad. Thank you for bringing me to Canada."

"You all know we aren't perfect," Sharon posted to social media. "But when I saw on the school's classroom wall the poem that Brendan—he's twelve—had written, it made my heart smile and I cried just a little."

WHAT HOME MEANS TO ME

What is great about my home? My house is very safe. Sometimes it's very annoying in our house. It's fun at our house. I never had a better home.

The home I have is safe. I like my house because it's safe. I am well fed and loved. My house is big and beautiful. I like it because I have a big family.

It's sometimes very annoying at my house. The little kids follow you everywhere. And how they yell in the house. It wakes up everybody when they have a day off. Well, that's how annoying my family is.

I have lots of fun with my family. I skate with my family and it's very fun. I also play board games with my family. It's also very fun playing Risk. Another thing that's fun is watching a movie with my family.

Now you know how it is in my home. As you can see my house is safe. Often my family is annoying but not always. Playing with my family is lots of fun. I never had a safer home.

Brendan

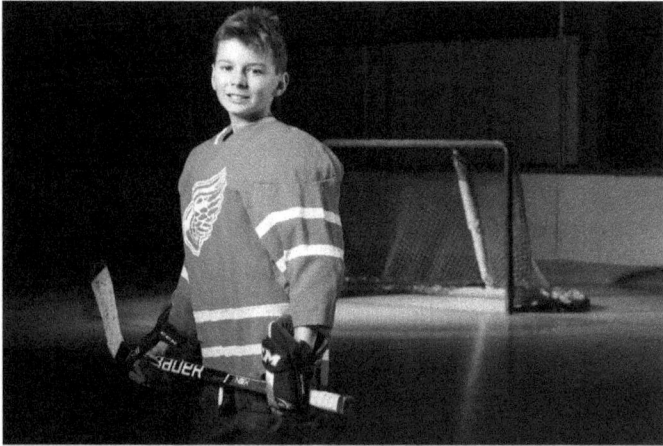

Declan, at his favourite sport - hockey. (like his brothers). He's come a long way from that 5-year-old stage where he wondered if there was a God out there somewhere. Or if prayer would help.

Little Meara, carving pumpkins. Just one more example of the family's everyday normalcy.

Portions of Christmas—See the family picture on the wall?

There's this strange thing that happens with kids. They grow up. Even adopted kids. Even Rob and Sharon's precious ones. And par for that journey is graduating from high school.

Graduation time at the family's house was fascinating in 2023. On June 28, two of their girls, Niamh and Sinead, were in the same class. Both graduated with the merit and laureate awards. Niamh won a scholarship that allowed her to go to college in the fall.

It was a time of celebration and giving thanks. And a time to be rightfully proud.

During the prep time, it felt a little bit like going too fast around a corner, considering the crucial amount of energy they had all put into Fallon's story, some of which was still ongoing. But the family determined to put all that aside and simply run with graduation as best they could, weary bodies notwithstanding.

The task of shopping for dresses fell into Sharon's lap. This was perhaps minor compared to the project Rob took on to secure their spot in the grad parade, a tradition at the high school. Every grad got to circle through town in a special, souped-up, or decorated vehicle of their choice. The parade entries were very diverse, including tractors, antique cars, rusty trucks, beat-up old buggies, and what-have-you. Rob, with the help of the girls and anyone else willing to pitch in, decorated his car with Ukrainian colours and symbols, displaying beautiful golden streamers, blue and yellow balloons, and a double-sided flag hoisted from the roof. There was also a platform for the girls to sit on, allowing them to wave at the many bystanders cheering them on.

Some aspects of graduation aren't about celebrations. It's also a coming of age period, a time to figure out who you really are and what you want to do with your life.

The two grads exemplified this. One wanted to move out and try life on her own. In fact, she already had a sort of decent job, so why not? The other wanted to stay close to home, save money, and go to college in the fall so she'd be able to achieve a better career down the road.

Neither of these divergent paths were wrong. They were just different.

By the way, the one who moved out still comes home for regular visits now and unexpectedly shows good appreciation for the opportunity!

• • •

The boys appeared to have a lot of "tall" genes in them. One by one, they shot way past Sharon and liked to remind her of it. And what boy doesn't take pride in saying, "I'm now taller than you, Dad"? Only Conor had achieved that one so far.

They also developed a penchant for sports. For Conor, it was basketball. He even played in the annual provincials tournament.

This past winter, three of the younger boys suited up in red to officially join the local minor hockey club. "Go, Red Wings, go!" Sharon yelled from the stands during games.

They may not have been heading for the NHL—not exactly, not anytime soon—but they enjoyed themselves.

And you can't raise boys without having first-car adventures. Or should we say misadventures?

"Sorry, Conor," a friendly neighbour teased. "I am not trying to spoil your secrets, but was it really only half a day you owned that car before its motor boomeranged on you?"

Thankfully, Rob was able to source an almost brand-new engine. Then he and Conor had some albeit greasy but good bonding time as he put his many skills to use to install the engine and get the car up and running again.

The car continues to run well.

Closing Words

As the story winds down, here are some final reflections. For example, is Fallon really okay now or will she continue to suffer? That question keeps being asked.

"It has both a yes and no answer," Sharon says. "But mostly the answer is, we don't know. Fallon is continuously under a doctor's care. She has constant checkups and undergoes many tests. We get frequent reminders that her numbers are sort of or even considerably 'off.' And yet she is also doing well. She enjoys school and has a high IQ. Except for some typical teenage angst, she is happy. So we trust her future to God. He knows. We don't have to know. Only time will tell."

Okay. And what about some final thoughts on adoption?

Sharon is deeply reflective on this subject, but it doesn't take long for her passion to rev up. She and Rob are inspired not to sit back anytime soon.

"Since the ongoing war in Ukraine, adopting from there isn't allowable now," she says. "But there are kids—lost, needy kids—in many other countries. Kids that are waiting... waiting for family, waiting for love, and perhaps waiting for you."

But she also has a warning.

"Don't go in with false expectations. Better still, go in with no expectations. There are no guarantees. Not when it comes to their health, no matter what the papers say. Not when it comes to their attitude, either. On the one hand, you see a kid's deep desire for love and family. On the other, it could take them years to learn to 'do' family well. A person's early damage tends to run deep. So if you go into adoption, go with a desire to love like Jesus loves. His love is unconditional, right?"

Family picture.

As one can imagine, Rob and Sharon have very few idle moments. But they do plan to answer any reader's questions if they should decide to reach out. They can be contacted by email (robandsharonsteeves@yahoo.ca), through Facebook Messenger (www.facebook.com/sharon.steeves.5), or by finding Sharon's blog (www.ittakesavillage.studio).

www.ingramcontent.com/pod-product-compliance
Lightning Source LLC
Chambersburg PA
CBHW071501070426
42452CB00041B/2076